Badass Likability

The Art of Making People Like You,
Building Charisma, Making Friends,
and Getting Things Your Way

Berger McDonald

Badass Likability

Copyright © 2018 by Berger McDonald

All rights reserved. No part of this publication may be reproduced, distributed, or transmitted in any form or by any means, including photocopying, recording, or other electronic or mechanical methods, without the prior written permission of the publisher, except in the case of brief quotations embodied in critical reviews and certain other noncommercial uses permitted by copyright law.

Information contained within this book is for entertainment and educational purposes only. Although the author and publisher have made every effort to ensure that the information in this book was correct at press time, the author and publisher do not assume and hereby disclaim any liability to any party for any loss, damage, or disruption caused by errors or omissions, whether such errors or omissions result from negligence, accident, or any other cause.

ISBN-13: 978-1-948040-15-0

First Edition: March 2018
10 9 8 7 6 5 4 3 2 1

Berger McDonald

CONTENTS

CONTENTS 3

INTRODUCTION 6

CHAPTER 1: WHAT DOES IT MEAN TO BE LIKABLE?
.... 12

CHAPTER 2: DON'T EVEN TRY 18

   THE SIGNS THAT YOU'RE TRYING TOO HARD 21
      Saying Yes All the Fricking Time 22
      Being on the Fence 24
      You Never Ask for Help 25
      You Have No Set Boundaries 26
      Forgetting Your Own Values 27
   NOT EVERYONE WILL LIKE YOU, NO MATTER WHAT 28
      Smell Ya Later, Hater 30

CHAPTER 3: WHY DOES SOMEONE LIKE YOU? 32

   WHAT'S IN IT FOR THEM? 34

THE ONLINE DATING CASE STUDY 37

CHAPTER 4: SWITCH YOUR TEAM 41

SIGNS OF TOXIC FRIENDS AND TOXIC PEOPLE 46
- *The Opportunist* 47
- *The Self-Centered* 49
- *The Victim* 51
- *The Super Clingy* 53
- *The Fakers* 54
- *The Over-Dominating Douche* 55

EASING YOUR WAY OUT OF THE TOXIC 56

CHAPTER 5: EIGHT SECRETS TO MAKE PEOPLE LIKE YOU 57

- *Your Powerful Weapon That You Probably Haven't Been Using* 60
- *"Fake it till you make it!" – Truth, or Bullshit?* 63
- *"Be a good listener" – Does It Really Work?* 67
- *Want People to be Interested in You?* 74
- *The Deepest Craving in Human Nature* 77
- *Kind vs. Clever* 80
- *Do This and Even Blind People Will Hate You* 82
- *What Is It That You Want From Her?* 85

CHAPTER 6: WHAT ABOUT ENEMIES? 91

- *Actions Speak Louder Than Words* 95
- *Build Your Supportive Team* 97
- *Tactfully Solicit Advice From The People* 99

Never Let Your Enemy Know You Are Onto Them 101
It's The Waiting Game 103

CHAPTER 7: MY SECRET OF ATTRACTION 105

WHAT KIND OF PEOPLE DO I NEED IN MY LIFE? 107
Someone Who's Always There 108
Someone Who Motivates You 109
Someone To Talk To 110
Someone Who Inspires You 111
Someone Who Is Honest 112
Someone Who Understands 113
MY SECRET OF ATTRACTION 115

FINAL WORDS 121

Introduction

"People seem to need a likable protagonist more than ever."

~Daniel Clowes, American cartoonist, novelist and illustrator

* * *

There was always that popular kid in school that everyone remembers. Maybe it was because they were funny, or good-natured to everyone, or they did a great impression of Homer Simpson. Something made others stand in awe.

That popular kid in school was even liked by the

teachers, parents of the other kids, and never once got pooped on by a bird. Even wild animals liked them.

Did you ever wonder what would that be like? To be liked? To be the most liked person ever?

Being liked doesn't always mean being popular, being liked means being accepted, respected and having a sense of belonging. The greatest social currency out there is being liked. This opens the door to many opportunities, such as getting invited to events, more people trusting you, nobody ever forgetting your birthday, or making your way through life much easier.

This book is about entering the world of likability— understanding how it can shape your future and give you the tools to harness your self-worth, purpose and identity.

We are embarking on a journey of self-discovery that delves into the meaning of being liked, things you should and shouldn't do in order to get there, and how learning the secrets to likability will give you the greatest chance at getting ahead.

But, is this book right for you?

I know you may be reading this with a growing heap of questions, such as whether you too can become more likable, or why would you even care to make others like you.

If that is the case, consider answering these questions:

- Do you want to be the person at work who always gets high-5s from everyone—even if you make a simple mistake like exploding the office?

- Do you want to be the husband or wife who always goes home to a cooked meal AND... hot sex?

- Do you want to be that friend who is always offered a drink as soon as his beautiful face shows up?

- Do you want to be the person who gets in everywhere for free—without using nudity or violence?

- Do you want to be the golden child of your parents and bask in the jealousy of your siblings?

- Do you want to live a happy life, knowing you're the best version you can be, and that the people around you are happy to be with you?

- Do you want to easily get things in life, your way, with little or no effort?

If you said yes to any of the questions above, then this book is definitely for you.

In this book, you will learn:

- **Why people like you.** Learn at the core level of human nature why people like others, so you can strategically make anyone like you, anytime you want.

- **What the majority of people are doing wrong**, and why they're wasting their time, why common advice such as *"be yourself,"* or *"be a good listener,"* or *"praise people,"* is not enough. See what you can do differently to step up your game.

- **The signs of toxic friends and other toxic people** around you. Those who won't truly like or support you, no matter what you do. And, most importantly, how to get rid of them.

- **How to handle enemies** without sabotaging your likable reputation, and always come out on top.

- **Learn the eight most powerful methods to make people like you.** Master these eight secrets and yes, you will become the most likable person you could ever imagine.

- **My #1 secret of attraction** to build charisma, make friends and have things go your way in life.

- And much, much more...

If any of the above resonates with you, then congratulations! You're about to enter the new world of endless opportunities, where you are the most happy, likable person you could ever be.

Turn to the next page and let the journey begin!

Chapter 1: What Does It Mean to be Likable?

"The greatest trap in our life is not success, popularity or power, but self-rejection."

~Henri Nouwen, Professor and Author of 'The Wounded Healer'

***

My friend Sam deleted her Facebook account one day, completely out of the blue. She was always the first person to comment on anything I posted, so I decided to call her up to find out what was wrong. I was worried that maybe she had blocked me for some reason, (we all get paranoid in these situations.)

"Hey Sam, are you okay?"

"Yes! Why wouldn't I be?"

"Well for starters, I can't see your Facebook account."

"Oh, yeah I deleted it. I'm so fed up of never getting comments or even likes. I made a drip cake the other day and uploaded 6 photos. I didn't even get a single like."

"That's uhm, heartbreaking. I'm sorry that happened to you."

"Well, I feel like nobody cares about me, or worse, my cakes."

"It's all about algorithms you know, most of your friends probably don't even see your feed. It's not because of your content."

"Can you explain that in English?"

"Jump back on Facebook and start interacting more

with friends you don't normally do, and soon you will see a change."

"Oh, okay, will do. By the way, did you watch the new season of Black Mirror?"

"No, sorry. Gotta go now. Write a post about it on Facebook and I will personally 'like' it. I might even leave a comment, too."

"Great, talk soon."

* * *

For Sam and many others out there, the idea of being liked and validated takes form on social media. People tend to gauge their popularity by the level of engagement involved. However, this isn't completely true or healthy.

If you spend a lot of time on social media, realize that there are a number of factors as to why friends don't interact, and some of it has nothing to do with you or what you post. It might come down to bad timing, other stuff in your friend's newsfeed or even if your friend has no Wi-Fi. They might even be at a funeral, or severely hungover, or crying in the bathtub eating chocolate. (Though if you are one of those people who constantly post mass-audience-orientated minion memes, I'd probably stop following you too.)

Of course there are other reasons too, such as:

- Posting offensive or gory pics

- Complaining all the damn time

- Uploading 1000 pics a day

- Tagging people in awful photos where they are drunk

But most importantly, the lack of attention you may get on social media doesn't reflect whether you are liked or not. Some of the greatest, most likeable people I know don't even have any social media account. On the other hand, I personally know some people who have thousands of followers on Facebook or Twitter, yet they're jerks in real life and everyone hates them.

* * *

So if social media isn't an indication of being liked, what is?

Technology does play a vital role in our everyday lives and has made communication a lot easier, beginning with the homing pigeon, but that doesn't mean phone calls, texts and emails serve as proof.

When you are liked, it affects every aspect of your life. You get the least workload at work, you get free craps wherever you go, and you even get invited to your friend's-dog's-girlfriend's birthday party. It's like you have a golden aura around you, so bright that everyone can't avoid looking into it.

You radiate this feeling of happiness and contentment that rubs off on other people just as easily.

Do you like Tom Hanks? Sure, he's made some awful movies, but he's a likable guy. There are stories of people who met Tom Hanks while he was on holiday in the Far East and he just smiled and signed an autograph. It's almost like a legendary story people tell over a campfire, that Tom Hanks really is the most likable person in the world.

And that's what will happen to you, once you begin to understand likability. You will find yourself with a wealth of benefits that will feel like something from a legendary story.

Chapter 2: Don't Even Try

"True friends stab you in the front."

~Oscar Wilde, incredibly famous poet and author

***

My friend Peter started working at a new company and decided that on his first day, he would make a great deal of effort to get everyone to like him.

As soon as Monday morning arrived, feeling refreshed and excited, Peter darted towards every new colleague he saw, offering a handshake and fake enthusiasm when they talked about their personal life. Though a little extreme, he was over enthusiastic to the point it seemed he would go as far as wiping their butts if that meant getting brownie points.

Peter's first day at work was coming to an end and as he looked around, he noticed that his new colleagues didn't seem that impressed with his efforts. In fact, they were avoiding him. Peter had initially gone in with high spirits but left feeling rather disappointed, and with low self-esteem. But Peter brushed it off as maybe the Monday blues, or that his new co-workers were severely hungover.

Over the course of the next several months, Peter kept trying hard to fit in. He would say yes to everything, agree to everything his co-workers said, and sometimes even worked overtime so the rest of the staff could enjoy happy hour, albeit without him. During this time, there was gossip about what a wimpy pushover he was, and he was the first person who got his hours cut during a difficult reshuffle in the office.

The problem with Peter was that he was trying too hard. No matter what he did—even letting the boss eat his delicious turkey sandwiches—he never got that big break he felt he deserved.

For Peter, there's got to be a different method to becoming likable. This will be explored later in the book.

The signs that you're trying too hard

Everyone wants to be liked, but wanting others to practically worship you is going too far. It might even come across as narcissistic or get you criticized for being an obvious people-pleaser.

You might be trying too hard in life as well but how do you really know? Luckily, there are a few signs that reflect your insatiable brown-nosing abilities.

Saying Yes All the Fricking Time

"Sure, I can stay and work late. My son doesn't really need to go to his soccer game tonight. It's just a final match, and he can try again next year"

"Sure, I will let you use my toothbrush. I only bought it today."

"Sure, I will give you one of my kidneys. I only need one after all."

"Sure, I will let you punch me in the face. Thanks so much, I really enjoyed that."

Really? Someone who says yes all the time is trying way too hard. Stop it right now. ALWAYS putting other's first can jeopardize other areas in your life. Especially the people you always say yes to usually are people who don't matter. Do you say yes to have lunch with a boring co-worker, but no to your grandmother's 90th birthday?

Saying yes is easy. There is no struggle, no conflict

or resistance, and you don't hurt anyone's feelings. The wimpy will say yes all the time to avoid confrontation. But the badass will stand up and say no when needed, so he can stay focused on what matters most. Remember you're a badass, so stop trying too hard, and stop saying yes all the fricking time.

Being on the Fence

Oh no, someone is discussing something controversial like whether or not pineapples should go on pizza. What should you do? Well, if you are trying too hard, you will straddle the fence and say, *"I don't know, it's too difficult to decide."* You are afraid of alienating someone, I get it, but the consequence is that nobody will ever take you seriously.

Force yourself to give an answer. Show everyone that you have an opinion whether it has a polarizing effect or not. Use some humor if you are really worried.

You Never Ask for Help

Although you will always help others, even if they don't ask for it, it is typically you that struggles to ask for help.

Remember that you aren't Chuck Norris and therefore can't do everything by yourself. Working as a team or delegating tasks helps build relationships and gives you opportunities to learn more about others. We have all worked in a job that involves some kind of monotonous routine, but the fact that you have someone else there softens the blow, and shares the misery.

You Have No Set Boundaries

Don't you just love it when the mother-in-law comes round and starts looking through your cupboards and drawers, occasionally playing hide and seek with your insulin? It's great isn't it, especially when she tells you to shut up and eat her over-cooked casserole?

You need to set boundaries, take back your power and don't let anyone take advantage of you. Commit yourself to speaking up and standing your ground.

Forgetting Your Own Values

Juggling the values of others along with your own is guaranteed to end in chaos. It's like you told your friend you stopped drinking for a month, only for them to peer-pressure you to come out.

Your values are most likely conflicting with someone you are trying to please. Each time you decide to stick to your guns and align with your own values, others may not be happy about it because they know how much of a push-over you are. Focus on spending your time and energy on yourself and not some awful douche. Look into ways of setting and attaining goals that are aligned with your own values.

Not Everyone Will Like You, No Matter What

Before diving into how to make people like you, there is a sad truth you need to accept. Not everyone is going to like you. Period. It doesn't matter how awesome you are, how beautiful you are, or if you own a chocolate factory, there are ALWAYS going to be haters.

The most successful people in the world aren't liked by everyone. Steve Jobs often got criticized for his attire. Mark Zuckerberg gets criticized for coming across like a robot, and while Richard Branson is good at playing the all-round good guy, he's always seems to be suing people.

It's the same for even the President of the United States. Do you like Mr. President? You do? Good, now go and ask any person you see the same question. One out of every two people will tell you they hate him. Look at the popular votes and you always see that close to 50% of the population dislike him. Some even hate him so much they make a career out of hating him.

You see, even famous, successful people, including the President of the United States, arguably the most powerful man on Earth, can't make everyone like them. Do you think you can? If you do, please stop, because you will be trying too hard.

Smell Ya Later, Hater

The term "hater" isn't just a word used by pretty teenage girls who don't get their way; it also describes people in this world who are full of hate. If you were to dissect a hater, you will wonder how long their heart has been both cold and black.

Haters take many different shapes and forms. It might be the neighbor hoping you step in their dog's poop which they "forgot" to clean up. It might be a relative who hates that you didn't take their offer to work at their cheese sandwich factory and hopes you fail in starting your own business. It might even just be some basement-dwelling internet trolls who are two cheeseburgers away from a heart attack.

Whenever you succeed or become perceived as popular, the haters appear from a thick fog. The idea that you are doing good makes them look bad. Sometimes the haters are people who used to like you, but are now jealous that you took the same risks that they could have taken, and you succeeded while they didn't, because of their inaction.

Haters won't like you. They hate you. Sometimes you think they hate you for no apparent reason, and you wonder why they do it. Why do they hate you? The most important answer to that question is this. Why should you care? Haters don't deserve even the whiff of one of your farts, let alone your sincere attention.

Your next step: Cut the haters out, and start by identifying three people who cause you the most pain in the butt, or other areas. You should write their names down to remind yourself to get rid of them.

Once you have enough courage to do so, do it! Block them on social media if you like, tell them you are going to stop hanging out with them if they are persistent, but better yet, to the extent possible, quietly ease out of their lives.

Chapter 3: Why Does Someone Like You?

"Old friends pass away, new friends appear. It is just like the days. An old day passes, a new day arrives. The important thing is to make it meaningful: a meaningful friend - or a meaningful day."

~Dalai Lama, Tibet's Political Leader, Activist and Religious Figure

***

In kindergarten, I remembered this kid named Yamato. His family was originally from Japan, and they moved to the US when he was two. He was a shy kid, and didn't speak much. None of the other kids ever spoke or noticed Yamato until one day he brought in a Gameboy with the latest Pokémon game—the one that wouldn't be released in the US until a year later.

Sure the game was in Japanese, but none of us cared. The TV show was a massive hit back then and all the kids eagerly surrounded him during recess. So, for a few months, Yamato was the most liked kid in school. Parents and teachers thought it was because of his good behavior, and subsequently gave him an award to recognize his awesome personality, documented for posterity by a photo with a confused Yamato smiling awkwardly.

But not too long after, yo-yos came into fashion—the ones with lights that flashed when they were whirled—and Yamato found himself alone again. One could imagine his disappointed parents quietly removing his award from the mantelpiece.

What's In It for Them?

Since that early kindergarten experience watching what happened to Yamato, I started to have a sad realization. That realization grew stronger as I grew older, and through observations in life, I've come to a sad conclusion.

Nobody gives a shit about you...

Yes, that is sad, but it is the truth, at least for the majority of people. Nobody really gives a shit about you unless there is something in it for them.

That popular girl I wanted to date back in high school didn't care if I thought she was pretty. She didn't give a shit if I'd been thinking about her all day or night. That didn't make her want to date me. What she cared about was what I could bring to the table that she valued. Was I good looking? Was I interesting? Did I have a car? Did I have anything that was attractive to her? That was all in it for her.

Your boss doesn't give a shit if you don't show up for work. He doesn't care if you are sick, or what may have happened to you. But he does care that your absence may make his job more difficult. He's not necessarily an asshole—it's just that he has his own worries to deal with.

People care about themselves and if a particular situation or person can give them something advantageous. When a stranger gives you directions while you are lost, it's not really because they care about you. They do so because it makes them feel good. They enjoy the feelings of helping someone else.

So without putting something out there, something to offer, you don't get anything in return. If you want to make someone like you, think about what you have to offer that is valuable to them. Maybe not a Gameboy with the latest Pokémon game, but maybe an interesting friend to cheer up their lives, should you happen to be funny or knowledgeable, or have never lost a game of beer pong. What is it that you can give?

If you are interested in asking someone out on a date, what do you have that they might like? Is it a car? Are you attractive? Can you do an outstanding Chewbacca impression?

If you want someone to like you to earn some business, or gain respect as a professional, think of what it is that they value, and whether you can give it to them?

The Online Dating Case Study

You know why online dating works so well? No, it's not because everyone is socially-inept these days. Well, maybe a little.

In a nutshell, you can write up an introduction that gives a little insight into you as a person. The things that interest you, your beliefs and ambitions, your hopes and dreams can all easily be identified by someone who feels the same way or relates to you.

Back in the day when I was in the dating game, I usually liked to include that I was a big Spiderman fan, even though I was in my late 20s. Some people might have been put off by this, but then I got a message from someone who was also a Spiderman fan, and next thing you know, we were talking about how much we hate Tobey Maguire and how far I could shoot my web.

It's not enough these days to just write, "I'm a fun person," on your dating profile. What the heck does that even mean? Remember, if your online dating profile is blank, it's no wonder why nobody wants to date you. Surprisingly, a photo of a garden isn't sexy or interesting enough to attract a date.

A long time ago, we used to be able to understand our greatest traits from reading our horoscopes or talking to a drunken friend, when they are their most honest, of course. But nowadays, it seems much more of a challenge, but really you've just got to find the common ground.

Finding the common ground means that conversation isn't a tricky minefield full of fake laughs and awkward silences. That the only thing to talk about is the weather, or if you got anything stuck in your teeth after the meal.

People are attracted to those they have things in common with, or qualities that make them admirable. Take a moment to think about your friends—you know, the family you get to choose—and think about which of your qualities that they love.

Are you the ringleader of the group? Do you come out with taboo jokes? Can you fit your entire fist into your mouth? What makes you truly stand out, and in essence, be a likeable person?

If you don't have any friends, think about what qualities your family or pets tolerate instead.

Make a list of your most positive traits and take a moment to reflect on these. Now, whenever you are trying to impress someone, do any of these traits come out?

If you are a generous person, does this show when you are trying to be liked? If you are a funny person, are you telling jokes, or are you thinking about the jokes that you will tell instead? If you are a polite person, are you being overly polite when you meet a new person?

***

So how does a person like you? It's either because there is something in it for them, or that you both share a common ground.

Take a moment to think about this and then move on to the next chapter. You're now ready to take the first step to make yourself a likable person.

Chapter 4: Switch Your Team

"The thing I love most about my job is watching people age backward, becoming more lively and energetic as they free themselves from situations that are toxic to their essential selves."

~Martha Beck, Sociologist, Life Coach and Author.

* * *

Remember my poor friend Peter from the earlier chapter, the guy who was trying too hard at work?

Peter spent a lot of time with people who never

really appreciated him, in fact, they disliked him. Yet, Peter was oblivious, and each time they belittled him, whether publically or online, he assumed he needed to try harder to please them. At work, Peter would be running errands during his spare time, and in his social circle, he was the first person to buy the rounds on a night out, frequently the only one to buy rounds. Even his family would scrutinize and abuse Peter to the point that he would spend a fortune on gifts in an attempt to appease them.

For Peter it seemed like there was no light at the end of the tunnel. It seemed like this vicious cycle of verbal diarrhea he so often tolerated was never ending. The outcome was that his mental wellbeing suffered, his self-esteem diminished significantly, and he took solace watching Disney movies because the happy endings gave him comfort.

Then one day, Peter was watching an episode of the Oprah Winfrey show about someone he could relate to. He sat glued to the screen as the woman being interviewed blubbered out the list of the assholes in her life.

"Yes!" Peter thought, *"I know that feeling!"*

Oprah interjects subtly, like a waiter recommending the special dish of the day.

"You need to get rid of these toxic people, and find people who care and love you."

Peter knew that this was a sign, especially considering the fact he couldn't find the remote and normally never watched Oprah. It was his epiphany moment. This moment felt like divine intervention and a wake-up call to make a change.

Peter decided that he would no longer try so hard to please everyone. Instead he would focus on the people who actually like him. He quit his job even though there were half-assed protests from colleagues who realized they would have no-one to walk over anymore. No longer would Peter feel the need to run to Starbucks in the pouring rain or smile when a nasty co-worker purposely farted as they walked past his cubicle.

Peter found a new job and a new mindset accompanied him. He would disengage in awkward conversations about politics, and he earned respect. He said no to anyone who begged him to go get a coffee or sample his turkey sandwich, and he earned greater respect. He was the real deal and not just someone with sex appeal.

By acknowledging that the people around him were toxic, he switched his team and found a new job with new co-workers; people who actually shared the same interests as he did, and Peter soon discovered he was being himself. Peter no longer settled for coming across as the desperate brown-noser with no backbone, but instead was just a genuine guy, and his co-workers appreciated that.

So, before trying to make people around you like you, switch your team. Get rid of all the toxic people first. What you're left with are the great people that you can start to make friends with, and have them grow to like you for the right reasons.

Sometimes we have no idea that we are surrounded by toxic people and we end up overcompensating for their approval. We try to impress them, buying presents or letting them borrow things they never give back. Eventually, one day you will snap and go nuts, leading to a Wild West style confrontation, perhaps armed with handbags.

This is why it's imperative to be able to follow these steps:

1. Identify toxic friends and toxic people in general.

2. Ease your way out of their life.

3. Find better people to surround yourself with.

Signs of Toxic Friends and Toxic People

Friendship isn't always about loyalty, support and juicy gossip. Friends can be hard to read once in a while, though the frequency and level of this behavior can tell you something isn't right. You need to identify what this person is really up to and whether you need them in your life.

To do this, you need to look out for certain traits that are like flashing beacons warning you.

The Opportunist

These are the type of friends or people who only like you because of what you have, such as your car, lots of money or a pet elephant. They might be using you to get close to one of your friends, a family member, or work associate, and when confronted, they become angry.

They will constantly attempt to borrow money, your clothes or even your toothbrush. They will probably let others use your belongs too, and won't even bother to ask if it's okay. Every time you have something new, they appear from the shadows with eagerness, and their ears flapping harder than Dumbo. Expect a battery of lies as they attempt to get your goods or whatever it is that they want.

Friend: *"Hey, haven't seen you in ages. I saw online you bought a new mountain bike. Mine is broken. Could I borrow yours? My family is going to, erm, Mount Everest."*

You: *"But there's no bike trails there?"*

Friend: *"Oh, I mean, I'm doing a charity ride."*

You: *"Oh, which charity?"*

Friend: Pauses, looks around and sees a stray dog. *"The stray dog charity!"*

You: *"Okay, here is the bike. Uhm, wait, but don't you hate dogs? Remember my cat you stole?"*

The Self-Centered

The self-centered don't hesitate to inform you about every aspect of their life, without you even getting a word in. They aren't interested in anything about your day or how you feel. They brag a lot, brag about materialistic things or their next trip on holiday in their camper van. They are always one-upping anything you say in conversation. They know everything while flaunting their opinion, but have no empathy whatsoever.

You: *"My grandmother just passed away."*

Friend: *"Oh, my grandmother died when I was 11."*

You: *"I am so sad right now. I was really close to her"*

Friend: *"My grandmother practically raised me."*

You: *"Her funeral is tomorrow. I'm nervous about getting through it."*

Friend: *"I couldn't go to my grandmother's funeral*

because it was also my birthday. That was when I got my first pony."

The Victim

The victim is someone who is constantly exuding how miserable their life is. They only come to you when they need help, and they over-exaggerate how much hardship they are going through. But when you need advice or help, they seem to never be around. They can only accept their point of view and usually start a story with "OMG," or "I can't believe." They seriously crave attention and always attempt to steal the spotlight.

You: *"Hey, I just got a raise. I'm so happy right now. Let's go get something nice tonight."*

Friend: *"—"*

You: *"Hello? Are you listening?"*

Friend: *"Oh my God, I can't believe my boyfriend hasn't texted me back!"*

You: *"When did you last text him?"*

Friend: *"Five minutes ago, oh no wait. Sorry, two minutes ago."*

You: *"Oh, maybe he's just busy, like on a phone call or something. Two minutes isn't long."*

Friend: *"HE'S HAVING AN AFFAIR. I just know it"*

The Super Clingy

The clingy friend is a lot like wearing a thong, occasionally fun but stuck right up your butt in no time. They don't want you to have anybody else. If you are going on a date, they somehow magically appear out of nowhere and sit next to you, eating food off your plate and obnoxiously talking over the conversation. They only say or do things to get recognition for themselves. As soon as they find a significant other of their own, you can expect them to ditch you.

Friend: *"So, what are we doing tonight?"*

You: *"Oh, I'm meeting my boyfriend."*

Friend: *"Great, what time are we going?"*

You: *"I am going at seven, it's our anniversary."*

Friend: *"Ah, so the place you first met? See you there."*

The Fakers

You think that fakers belong only in high-school but unfortunately they manifest into adulthood too. Polite to your face but always talking crap about you behind your back. They promise to call or see you but never do, always keeping you waiting. They make up lame excuses and never keep their promises. One of their main hobbies is gossip.

You: *"Hey, so it's my birthday tomorrow, are you coming to the party?"*

Friend: *"Ouch, I can't. I have a thing."*

You: *"What thing?"*

Friend: *"I mean, I have work."*

You: *"I thought you were self-employed?"*

Friend: *"Yes, but I got a big order today—a dog wedding."*

The Over-Dominating Douche

This is the type of friend or person who dominates everything. They won't even let you sneeze without you asking their permission first. They have massive insecurities and will constantly pull you down. It might be a manager at work or a family member who thrives on the idea that you don't have the courage to stand-up to them. They are influential among others, and might be able to turn other people against you, and essentially ruin your life.

Friend: *"What are you doing?!"*

You: *"I'm editing my resume for that job at the new Mexican restaurant."*

Friend: *"I wouldn't bother, you won't ever get that job"*

You: *"Why not?"*

Friend: *"You know nothing about Mexico."*

You: *"Thanks for the support"*

Easing your way out of the toxic

Now you should be able to effectively identify who is really not worthy of your awesomeness. The next thing is getting them out of your life without resorting to a restraining order, or a blowtorch.

Making a decision on which friendships are worth continuing is difficult, but if someone makes you question yourself, saps your energy and enthusiasm, or uses your resources regularly without returning the favor, then it's time to cut them out.

If they aren't too bad, and if you can't avoid them completely, just downgrade them from friend to acquaintance, such as people at work or family, otherwise if there are no formal links to your life, you should break the bond entirely.

Chapter 5: Eight Secrets to Make People Like You

"Popularity isn't just something that happens. You have to give something in exchange for it, and that's the dangerous part of the process."

~Robert Bringhurst, Canadian poet, typographer and author.

***

After you've dispensed with the toxic people in your life, and have identified the type of people you want to hang out with, now it's time to get to the good part—making people like you.

Ever heard of Hugh Hefner? The famous old man who had like a hundred girlfriends and lived in a mansion? So, he did have a huge fortune, but he was also likable. He was as real as you could get—aside from his daily need for Viagra. Hugh offered more than just superficial looks, money and fame. Every heterosexual man on the planet wanted to be him, but would never have the personality traits that made him likeable.

The truth is, to get someone to like you doesn't necessarily involve money, fame or deteriorating sex appeal. It might simply be shared interests, like a hobby you both enjoy, or being avid collectors of something obscure, such as celebrity toe nails.

So, how do you make someone like you? Can you make someone like you by using a fishing rod and dangling a $10 bill above their head? The answer is a lot simpler than you imagine.

Master the following methods, and you are sure to make even a most hateful person like you. By the way, that hateful person should be on your toxic list and already eliminated in the previous chapter. But in the event you meet someone new, say at work, you'll have the opportunity to try out these powerful methods you're about to discover.

Your Powerful Weapon That You Probably Haven't Been Using

The simplest, yet most powerful weapon to make people like you—**your smile**.

You must know someone who always smiles? Are they someone you like? Think about the most likable person you personally know. Next time when you're with them, notice how often they smile.

Smiling is infectious; it breaks down barriers and offers others the chance to feel comfortable and happy. Smile as much as you can whenever you meet anyone. Of course you should temper your smile when appropriate, such as at a funeral, a serious business situation, or you hear some bad news.

Do you know anyone that hate babies? Babies are one of the most likable creatures on earth. Why is that? They smile! These tiny humans who are new to the world can bring so much joy—simply with a smile.

When a woman gives birth after hours of

excruciating pain, the moment she sees her baby smile she thinks, *"aww, that was so worth it."*

You could be at an emergency room with nobody talking, all angrily simmering inside because they've had to wait so long. People are in pain and itching for an opportunity to explode. But then, someone brings in a baby, and the toothless grin will melt the hearts of even the most annoyed old man there.

Dogs are the same; they get away with so much crap in day to day life. They steal your socks, hump your leg and drool all over your crotch—not unlike your crazy ex. You get angry, but when you look at those big eyes, that doggy smile and wagging tail, it's hard to stay mad. We humans don't have tails to wag and it's gross to drool all over anything. So to get people to like you, how about a smile? :)

<u>Your Next Step</u>: Smile more. Take a look in the mirror and practice your best smile. Spend one day smiling to everyone you meet and see how many people smile back. You will be surprised at how powerful a simple smile can be.

***

<u>Likability Secret #1</u>: Your smile. Smile more, smile often. Make it the first thing you do when you see people.

***

"Fake it till you make it!" – Truth, or Bullshit?

"Fake it till you make it!" I'm sure you've heard about this advice before. It's also bullshit advice I see from so many fake self-help gurus these days. If they advise you to "fake it", they might be fakers themselves, probably still living in their mom's basement, inflating their fake income numbers so they can trick you into buying their fake advice. If you come across one of them, don't take advice from that faking faker from Fakeville.

Remember when my friend Peter tried to *"fake it"* at his first job but never did *"make it?"* After he quit his job and got the new one, he decided to *"just be himself"* and things just worked out. This is when you see the advice of *"just be yourself"* come into play. Your values and beliefs are what make you distinct from everyone else, they are the core of who you are and by staying true, you will usually avoid ending up in moments of conflict. *"Just be yourself,"* helps you remember to never change your view to suit someone else.

Do you want people around you to be honest with

you? It's easy—don't fake or lie. It takes courage to stay true, but this is also how you weed out people you don't need in your life. It might make you unpopular at first, but it will attract others who feel the same way.

The problem with lying is that you have to remember your lies. You should aim to never tell a lie, as this kind of openness and honesty will draw people towards you. You'll come across as genuine and realistic, instead of fake or wishy-washy. Another problem with lying is that once you get a reputation for it, everything you say becomes suspect. If you always tell the truth, you'll be accepted at face value.

This "what you see is what you get" approach to making friends will drive away the assholes, like the ghost of Edgar Allen Poe. Just remember not to appear inflexible, as people might think you are rigid.

Be aware that, *"just be yourself"* doesn't work if you use it the wrong way. For example, if you're one of those annoying people who complain all the time, or always criticize or find fault with others, and choose to *"just be yourself"* instead of making positive change to improve yourself, don't be surprised if you find yourself alone. In this case, *"just be yourself,"* can result in *"all by yourself"* with no one to love.

Your next step: Try to practice being open and honest, even when you feel uncomfortable or frustrated. Explain how something makes you feel in honest, non-confrontational way.

* * *

Likability Secret #2: Staying true and always being honest

* * *

"Be a good listener" – Does It Really Work?

You've probably heard the common advice of *"Being a good listener."* Does it really work? Can being a good listener make people like you?

Let's talk about my poor friend Peter again. Don't worry, this is the last time we talk about him in this book.

Peter managed to get a new job after he had cultivated a new mindset. This mindset helped him become a confident badass. He gained respect, and was no longer being awkwardly ignored in the elevator at work, even if was trapped inside for six hours! While things were better than ever, there was still one aspect of his life that he struggled with—dating.

Peter was profoundly perplexed at finding a partner. He was good looking, had a great job with great pay, owned a house *and* a car, yet no woman was interested after a first date.

Badass Likability

He called me for help, and as a good friend, or so I thought, I decided to help him.

On a side note, this happened way before I wrote my book **"Secret of Not Giving a F*ck"**. If you read that book, you would know this situation is what I call taking someone else's monkey and putting it on *your* back. Having a "monkey on your back" mean you're carrying a burden—a monkey—on your back all the time. It's hard enough to get rid of your own monkey, but from time to time, you unconsciously take on other people's monkey too. In this case, Peter gave his monkey—his dating problem—to me, and I took it, even though I had my own dating problem to worry about. Anyway, back to the story.

I introduced Peter to my friend Sam. Remember Sam—the girl who deleted her Facebook account? I genuinely thought they would really hit it off, plus I promised Sam she could use my Netflix account for a week. Surely a win-win situation, right?

Peter told me that their date went extremely well and confided in me that he had found his soul mate. Oh boy, what was I thinking? However, Sam refused to get in contact with him, and even refused to go on a second date.

Very confused, Peter asked for help again. He wondered if she was simply playing hard to get since she had blocked him on social media and ignored his calls. He asked me to check on Sam to see what was wrong.

So, I called Sam, and she stated that she was interested in Peter initially. He was attractive and seemed to be fairly stable. It wasn't until Sam realized that Peter hadn't given her a moment to talk about herself that the interest significantly dwindled.

"The whole time he kept talking about himself—his hobbies, his house, his car and his stuff. He never let me have a chance to talk about myself, let alone...my cakes," Sam said.

Sam wanted a man who cared about her, and not just himself. She said she would prefer to go on a date with a robot, at least there would have been an "off" button. Sam wondered if Peter put up a dating profile from craigslist, because his narcissism and ego-centric demeanor matched that kind of profile.

Peter soon learned that while he might get every tick for the check-list of being a good guy, none of that mattered if he couldn't listen. He didn't talk with Sam, he talked *at* her.

So, poor Peter now realized the importance of being a good listener. It was even vital to his ability to find someone. Peter resolved that the in the future when he went on a date, he would curb the constant talking and put emphasis on listening instead. This new tactic eventually led to Peter finally finding someone.

* * *

Most of us think we are good listeners; all you have to do is sit there, blink occasionally and use 4-syllable adjectives near the end to show you've been paying attention such as *"fascinating*!" or *"extravagant*!"

But there is much more to it than that. If you are

a good listener, people will feel motivated to talk to you, and as a result they will like you. However, becoming a good listener takes lot of practice, too.

Therapists make it look easy, or so we think; but there are a number of things they are doing that make them good listeners. Such as:

- They give their undivided attention. They aren't pissing around with their phone, playing Candy Crush or practicing yoga while you talk.

- They use their body to show intent, leaning in closer when you talk, as if they're waiting for the punchline of a joke.

- They are patient. When there is a pause in conversation, they aren't using it as an opportunity to say something themselves, or ask to go to the toilet. This allows the other person time to find their words.

- They aren't thinking of their response

while listening. Only when the other person has finished speaking, then the therapist provides their input.

Some of the greatest leaders in the world—such as Richard Branson, Mark Zuckerberg and Willy Wonka—are all great listeners. This in turn encourages others to talk and makes them likable people. You can be a likable person, too, simply by listening intentionally.

Your next step: Try your best not to interrupt or compete. I know it's tempting when people are talking about something really exciting, like knitting or the thrilling hobby of stamp collecting, but try to wait for them to finish before you chime in.

When you are in a conversation, remember to talk less and listen more. Train yourself to invest in what someone has to say. By the way, this doesn't mean sitting on their lap and stroking their hair.

Likability Secret #3: Listen more and encourage others to talk about themselves.

* * *

Want People to be Interested in You?

Do you like car salesmen? Do you know anyone who does? The odds are slim, because generally speaking, everyone hates car salesmen. But that's not the case for David, another friend of mine.

David worked as a used car salesman at his dealership and he was great at it, breaking sales records all the time. Many clients loved David and bought cars from him over and over again. They constantly referred friends and family to him and as a result, David earned a fortune, even more than his own boss. What was his secret? Did David throw in a free set of silver fish knives? Was he dressed as a clown and making balloon animals?

When a prospective client walked in, the first thought of the other salesmen was this. *"What sales tactic should I use to squeeze the most out of this victim?"* all the while, calculating their commission in their heads.

But David was different. His first question to himself always was, *"What can I do to **help** this* *man/woman/family?"* He listened, learned about his client's needs and was genuinely interested in their needs, concerns, worries and doubts. He wasn't forcing a sale on them, he was showing honest interest.

He told me his secret. *"Every day before going to work, I remind myself that I love my clients. I listen to their needs, and recommend to them the car that I would personally choose, at the fair price that I would personally pay."*

David gained the trust of his clients because he showed his genuine interest in helping them, and in return they grew to trust him. He was putting them first and seeing them as people he loves, not numbers, or victims like the other snake oil salesmen.

People are not stupid. They know if you are genuinely interested in them, or if you're faking. So, to make someone like you, be genuinely, truthfully interested in them.

Your next step: When you want someone to like you, ask them questions and learn about their needs and wants in life. Tell them you are there for them, and mean it.

Sometimes we might have someone at work or in life who we think doesn't like us, but if you show interest and talk to them, things will change. Try asking someone for coffee and give them the stage to rant or moan, and listen with undivided attention and unrelenting eagerness.

* * *

<u>Likability Secret #4</u>: Being truthfully interested in other people.

* * *

Berger McDonald

The Deepest Craving in Human Nature

"The deepest principle in human nature is the craving to be appreciated." ~ William James

The quote above relates to our need to feel validated and important. Alex came across this quote while reading a book during his break time at work. It got him thinking about his wife who stayed home all the time. He realized he'd been taking her for granted for too many years and not appreciating all the things she sacrificed for him, and for the family. She put up with so much of his shit, and Alex realized that he should make more effort to show her how important she was to him. Why should he wait until Christmas, Valentine's Day, or her birthday, which he often missed, to show her how important she was to him?

Alex bought some flowers, wrote a note, and as soon as he arrived home, surprised her at the dinner table. He told his wife how much he appreciated her, how sorry he was for not showing his love for her, and promised her that from that moment forward, he would show his love for her each and every day.

She was astonished and overjoyed with emotion, sobbing hysterically. She later showed him a divorce letter she had been drafting, confiding in him how miserable she had been feeling. Alex then started sobbing hysterically, too. This simple act of appreciation saved his marriage because he made his wife feel important and validated.

Your next step: Next time someone does something for you, no matter how big or small, look into their eyes, smile, and say *"Thank You."* Show them how much you appreciate them, and you will notice the difference.

Make a list of three people you think you've been taking for granted, and make a plan to show them how important they are to you. Practice looking for the good characteristics of others in your life and make a valiant effort to show them how important they are.

***

<u>Likability Secret #5</u>: Make others feel they are important and appreciated

***

Kind vs. Clever

Jeff Bezos was precocious as a kid. Jeff spent one summer with his grandparents when he was 10. One day, Jeff was sitting in the back of his grandparent's car when he overheard on the radio that every puff of a cigarette takes minutes off your lifespan. An observant Jeff knew that his grandmother was a smoker and decided to calculate the number of years she could have taken off her life so far.

He told her that at 2 minutes per puff, she had already taken nine years off her life. Expecting his grandmother to be amazed by his wit and intellect, she burst into tears instead. His grandfather took him outside and told him, *"Jeff, one day you'll understand that it's harder to be kind than clever."*

What would you choose? Kind or Clever? Looks like Jeff had both. Maybe you got this book from Amazon? I'm sure if you ever have to deal with their customer service, you'll be impressed at how great and kind their customer service staff is.

The early lesson from his grandfather shaped

Jeff's life. He founded Amazon, innovating and leading in so many areas, and changing so many lives. At the time of this writing, he had just surpassed Bill Gates to become the richest man in the world.

Your Next Step: Be aware of situations in which you may hurt someone's feelings. Always aim to be kind instead, and you will notice a huge difference.

* * *

Likeability Secret #6: Be Kind

* * *

Do This and Even Blind People Will Hate You

Nicky was a beautiful blonde I used to work with years ago. She seemed to have all the characteristics every man dreamed off. She was beautiful, didn't get involved in office gossip, worked hard, was a caring person, and despite the blonde stereotype, was really smart. But instead of being a likable person, everyone in the office seemed to try to avoid her. Why? There was this one problem. She, well, had a pretty strong body odor.

If you smell bad, even blind people will hate you. Dogs will try peeing on you and nobody wants to sit next to you on the bus. You don't want to be that person! When you look good and smell good, you feel good. And people around will appreciate both your beauty and...your smell.

Showering regularly and keeping your home and car clean shows that you not only care about your health and body, but you care and respect the people around you. Use deodorant or antiperspirant when necessary, as strong body odor makes people run away from you like running away from a zombie.

And don't forget about your teeth. Unless it's made of gold, people don't want to talk to someone with yellow teeth or bad breath. No-one can get close to you if you have stinky breath.

For Nicky, I bet one of her friends must have finally gotten the courage to break the news to her one drunken night. Because one day, she came in the office, smelling like a rose. The next day she smelled like the fragrance of honeysuckle vines. Regardless, from that day on, she always smelled good and people immediately surrounded her as if she was Jessica Alba. She soon earned all the respect she long deserved.

Your next step: Have a vigorous hygiene regime, if you are going to be away for some time, make sure you have mints, gum or deodorant spray. Ensure you are looking good so you can feel good, and thus become more approachable.

* * *

Badass Likability

<u>**Likability Secret #7**</u>: **Maintain good hygiene**

* * *

Berger McDonald

What Is It That You Want From Her?

I remember one summer day, my grandma paid us a visit. My mom was busy that day, so grandma took me to the doctor's office for my annual checkup. When we arrived, there was already a bunch of other parents and kids waiting impatiently. As always, Mrs. Wilson was sitting at the reception counter. I wasn't sure how long she had been working at that office, but she was there since the first time my parents took me there as a child. For all those many years, I never saw Mrs. Wilson smile. She seemed to be very serious, sometimes even rude, and to be honest, I was a bit scared of her and the look in her eyes.

When we were at the counter, after checking me in, my grandma smiled at Mrs. Wilson and made a comment.

"You have beautiful eyes! Ever since I was a teenage girl, I always dreamed of having beautiful eyes like yours." Mrs. Wilson seemed to be surprised. She looked up, and made eye contact with Grandma—something I'd rarely seen her do. But most surprisingly—and for the first time in my life—I saw Mrs. Wilson crack a smile.

"Well, with all the wrinkles starting to form around my eyes, I don't look as good as I used to," she said.

Grandma reassured Mrs. Wilson, *"Maybe so, but they are still magnificent."* This time, Mrs. Wilson brought up an even bigger smile and said, *"When I was young, people really admired my eyes and my beauty. I won Miss Beauty Pageant in high school!"*

I had witnessed Mrs. Wilson smile, not once, but twice, within minutes. It was something that I never expected to see in my life. On the way home, I told grandma I'd never seen Mrs. Wilson that cheerful. Everyone here knew she was the most serious person and never smiled. My grandma replied that she'd just told her the truth. She truly believed Mrs. Wilson had beautiful eyes, so she complimented her.

"But why you do that? What is it that you want from her?" I asked.

"Nothing, kid. I thought her eyes were beautiful, so I let her know. She seems to be happy to hear that, and it makes me happy, too," my grandma said.

What is it that you want from her? Life is not a bunch of business transactions that we have to plan out and do all the calculations ahead of time, before we do something for someone. If we're that selfish and calculate what we can get out of the other person before we do anything for them, it should be no surprise that we'd find ourselves living a stressful, miserable and unhappy life we fully deserved.

I bet that Mrs. Wilson would be living on a cloud that day. She would go home happy. She would even smile at her husband and tell him about it. Thinking about it now puts a smile on my face. And I hope it puts a smile on yours, too. It's no wonder that my grandma was a very likable person. Everyone loved and respected her.

Happiness is not about fame or money, but it could be about making an impact on the people around you. When you make others happy, their happiness could be infectious and make other people happy to, including yourself.

Amanda, one of my readers, emailed and told me my book "**Secret of Not Giving a F*ck**" has given her the courage to leave the mundane job she has been doing for eighteen long years to pursue her dream, and my other book **"Badass Self-Discipline"** would be the motivator she needed for her to reach her new goals. It really made my day. If my books help just one person see the light at the end of the tunnel and keep pushing forward until success is achieved, then my day is a success as well. And I believe you would feel the same way too. You could use your words to make people happy, and you will be happy in return.

Words can be a deadly weapon and words can cut like a knife. On the other hand, words can also transform people, transferring a caterpillar into a beautiful butterfly. The best part is that words don't cost you a dime. So instead of hurtful, mean and critical words, how about compliments? Your words do not need to be big, fancy, or profound. Heck, your words don't even need to be grammatically correct, they just need to be genuine and sincere.

Compliments will get you everywhere in life, or close enough. When you are making comments that are genuine and specific, it brings others closer to you. When you make people happy, you are happy, and in the process, you make yourself likable.

But what if that person has nothing good to warrant a compliment? Yes, it is hard at first, and some people seem to not have any good characteristics at all. But just like Mrs. Wilson, every person has something good about them. The more you practice looking for the good in others, the better and easier it will get.

Focus on comments that emphasize someone's personality rather than their situation, for example. So you might say, *"Wow, you are so brave!"* instead of, *"You stopped that fall with your face!!!"*

Your next step: Everyone loves a nice surprise, whether that is a compliment, gift, or just a hug or pat on the back. Next time you see someone, try to find something good about that person and sincerely praise them. My challenge for you is to do this until you put a smile on their face.

Badass Likability

Likability Secret #8: Look for the good from other people, and give sincere compliments

* * *

Chapter 6: What about enemies?

"You must not fight too often with one enemy, or you will teach him all your art of war."

~ Napoleon Bonaparte, French statement and military leader

***

Despite how likable or beautiful you are, and what a compassionate human being you've become, there is a great chance you will come across an enemy at some point in time.

Enemies are simply haters that you know. They

make no attempt to hide their disdain for you and actively plan to sabotage your success whenever possible. Enemies probably spend more time thinking about you than their own happiness. Enemies usually don't like you, or worse, really hate you. Their hobbies include making a voodoo doll out of you, spreading malicious rumors about you, and leaving flaming bags of dog poop on your front porch. Enemies are sometimes unavoidable.

My cousin Lisa was a personal trainer and fitness vlogger living in a small rural town. Since she lived in a small town, everyone knew her and knew that she'd had three kids before becoming a personal trainer. Every Friday night, Lisa taught Zumba classes, but some of the other women at the gym hated what she did. They were jealous, and they thought someone who has had kids shouldn't have been so fit, and shouldn't have been able to lose the weight, toning and sculpting the body so beautifully.

One night, someone had drawn, uhmm, penises all over Lisa's Zumba posters. Lisa was distraught and as she looked around she identified the culprits—two other women standing by the water machine, giggling childishly. The brutal vandalizing of her posters was only the beginning, as the haters didn't get the reaction they wanted, so they wanted to push even further.

The haters started leaving bad reviews on Lisa's Facebook page, encouraging other people to not attend her classes, and shouted her name while she tried to do a squat.

What should Lisa do?

* * *

Yes, having enemies in your life is extremely daunting. There's that horrible feeling because you can't anticipate what the crazy bastards will do next. When we have an enemy, what we frequently want is revenge.

If they are spreading rumors, you may want to do the same to them, but elaborate more. If they are giving you "evils" across the room, you may want to salute them with the middle finger.

You get the idea, when we get mad we want to get even, but think about how that might affect you personally, as well as other's opinions of you. The greatest victory over our enemies requires no battle, retaliation or revenge.

So how do you deal with enemies?

Enemies are not always recognizable, often hiding under the cloak of niceness, but they will show their true colors in time.

Like when you learn that someone who you assumed was your friend is not, but now they have collected all your secrets like the villain in a James Bond movie.

No matter what you do, you can't avoid the presence of an enemy in your life, but there are ways to deal with them—not involving any sort of physical violence.

Actions Speak Louder Than Words

The enemy's main objective is to place you in harm's way. They literally don't care that they ruin your career or your life. When faced with lies that deliberately undermine your character or history, your gut instinct is to address the lies. You feel like generating as much evidence as you can to anyone who will listen, but this will futile.

For example, back in middle school, the moment I said to everyone, *"I did not make love to a chicken,"* immediately after such rumors surfaced, I began to look guilty. Especially when I also avoided eating chicken at lunch or refused to dance to the chicken song.

Words could be cheap but actions are evidence. Prove the enemy wrong by showing everyone how the lies are unfounded. Show people who matter how amazing you are and grab as much spotlight as possible, emphasizing your greatest qualities.

Work harder than ever before, come up with projects, offer free help and become awesome. There are always better things to be doing than spending time worrying about your enemy.

Eventually the lies will disappear and anyone who heard them will automatically know they are untrue, since the evidence of how well you are doing is clearly before them.

So don't engage, do the opposite. If someone throws the "chicken affair" rumor at you, do the chicken dance, joke about how much you really love chickens, and change your profile picture to a beautiful, red rooster with a heart emoji in the corner.

Build Your Supportive Team

Another great way to deal with enemies is building a supportive team around you. This will come in handy, especially if you have enemies at work.

In some way, large or small, everyone in your office plays a role in your career, today and in the future. If you spend a moment to get to know the janitor, they might one day say something good about you if someone important is listening. Never underestimate the power of the janitor because anything you try to flush, they will flaunt.

You could even spend an afternoon helping a manager with boring paperwork, or bring lunch to the IT guy while he is untangling some cables. Tell senior staff funny jokes or take them to bingo. Cultivate an outgoing and friendly demeanor so that it becomes a daily habit, almost ritualistic.

The more people at work that know you, the more protection you have. When an enemy shows up, or if a rumor spreads, you are already shielded from your enemy with the added benefit of co-workers standing up for you.

Even if you don't know everyone in your organization, you will find that you have developed such a good reputation that others will already be aware of your existence. By getting to know everyone at a personal level, you will also gain lifelong professional allies and friendships, almost like having your own avengers with varying skills and contacts!

So, if you have an enemy at your organization who is telling everyone a malicious and extremely nasty rumor, such as you hate Star Wars, the majority of co-workers will stand up for you because they recognized it as bullshit. They know you enough to not believe everything they hear, and have the benefit of the knowledge of all the things you've talked about.

Tactfully Solicit Advice From The People

Remember, when it comes to enemies, don't engage with the bastard bullies, but do let others know what's going on. The problem is that you have to be tactical about it, otherwise you might be perceived as badmouthing or being a gossip.

It's all about actions rather than words, and people need to see that you are in harm's way without you having to show them.

So think of someone that you can trust to help you, and maybe ask them out for lunch, perhaps under the pretext of talking about Game of Thrones. Tell whoever you confide in that you don't necessarily dislike your enemy, but feel confused lately since they keep giving the middle finger or cutting the brakes of your car. Don't tell them your own conclusion or give the impression that you feel under attack.

When you are telling your story, include a few unrelated things as well, so that the sole purpose of the conversation wasn't about your enemy. This is challenging, because once you start talking about your enemy, the tendency will be to really go to town on them.

In this type of situation, indirect communication is key. No one ever believes someone who proclaims that they are under attack so you have to filter your own perspective. If you don't, you will look paranoid, evasive and might end up having to answer awkward questions about what's happened so far. No one wants a confrontation with the mother-in-law.

State only facts without analysis, and provide your ally the idea that you have a willingness to fix the problem. This should be all you need to help your associate understand that you are indeed under attack without needing to say it, and hopefully they will help you.

Never Let Your Enemy Know You Are Onto Them

The old adage of "keeping your friends close but your enemies closer" is surprisingly accurate when dealing with enemies. If you engage with the enemy, it is almost guaranteed that things will escalate once they know you are aware of their nasty behavior.

The trick is to make them feel as if they are in control and that you have no idea they are attacking you. Treat your enemy like a best friend, ask them about their weekend and work life in an upbeat and enthusiastic way. If they attempt to belittle or undermine you, laugh it off or rephrase what they are saying back to them.

Enemy: *"You smell like taco sauce."*

You: *"I smell like taco sauce?"*

Enemy: *"Yes, sorry to tell you, but you needed to know."*

You: *"I thought I smelled like barbeque sauce today, but*

taco sauce is way better. Thanks buddy."

Enemy: *"Oh, erm, no problem."*

As Oscar Wilde once said, *"Forgive your enemy, nothing annoys them more."*

This helps give the perception that you are a tough nut to crack, that they need to try harder to break you, or that nothing they are doing is even working. If the enemy thinks you are aware of their efforts of sabotage, then they might turn up the heat.

If the enemy has no clue that you are on to them, they will eventually give up. The more they think you are dumb, the less of a threat you are.

It's The Waiting Game

The downfall of the enemy is due to their own hands, or words. Like getting caught red-handed spray-painting nasty stuff on the employee of the month wall. Vicious people always end up shooting themselves in the foot, harming their own reputation, and losing their own sense of self-respect.

You don't have to go down to their level, and why would you want to? What kind of person spreads rumors, leaves passive-aggressive notes everywhere and carries around a makeshift voodoo doll made from a Barbie?

Focus on building stronger connections with others instead of giving time to enemies. Don't take revenge or retaliate.

***

For my cousin Lisa, instead of giving the haters the reaction they wanted, Lisa chose a different approach. She ignored the haters, and instead, focused all her energy and effort on what she did best—training and motivating her clients to be in the best shape they could be.

Eventually her hard work paid off. She gained trust from her clients, and built a large fan base of enthusiastic gym members. The fake bad reviews on her Facebook page got buried by all the good, real reviews from her clients thanking her for all her hard work. Some of her fans even stood up for her to confront the haters. She has built a very strong foundation based on her genuine interest in helping her clients to get the results they wanted. Her business is now so solid that no amount of hate from the haters could sabotage her.

***

"The greatest victory is that which requires no battle."

~Sun Tzu, Author of The Art of War

Chapter 7: My Secret of Attraction

"By accepting yourself and being fully what you are, your presence can make others happy."

-Jane Roberts, American poet and author

The search and struggle to become accepted or liked throughout life seems never ending. We want to have the greatest friends, the warmest atmosphere at work, and the most wonderful people to love.

By now you should already know how to make

people like you. The hardest part is how to find all the great people to surround ourselves with.

It all starts with identifying the type of people you want to attract to your life.

What Kind of People Do I Need in My Life?

Take a moment to think about the type of people that you need in your life. Imagine you are telling them exciting news and you are envisioning their reaction. Are they overjoyed that you learned to tie your shoelaces? Did they jump on you like a tiger, giving you a firm, memorable hug? Did they offer to get you drunk to celebrate?

Pay attention to these little details, as they are indications if someone really likes you. Being likeable obviously comes with huge benefits, but you have to understand that having the right people in your life can only amply your beneficial personality traits.

So, what are you looking for in a person? Here are a few things to consider.

Someone Who's Always There

You are hungover and need food, or an alibi to avoid going into work. You have someone to help nurse you to health and imitate your voice when they call your office. You can tell them all the awful drunken things you did and they won't judge you.

They are always there, and always ready to lend you a hand in some way or the other.

Someone Who Motivates You

Quitting is for losers, unless of course you are a smoker, and in that case, please do. You need someone who lifts you up when you are feeling you can't achieve your dreams.

They won't allow you to quit, they will push you like a passive-aggressive personal trainer. They refuse to let you ever give up.

Someone To Talk To

You need someone who could potentially make a great therapist, but also someone you can really confide in who will never use anything you say against you. Talk about the complicated things in your life, or just let them hug you when you need to cry.

You can call them anytime and they are always willing to listen.

Someone Who Inspires You

They aren't afraid to talk about their problems or struggles, and in fact they anticipate occasional failure, which is why they have succeeded in life.

This is the kind of person who makes you feel like you too can better yourself and do anything with their support.

Someone Who Is Honest

No sugarcoating things with this person. If you need the right advice you will get it. Not only will they give you a reality check, but they will also help you figure out what to do next. They are telling you the truth, not because they are spiteful, but because they genuinely care about you.

A taste of tough love so that you can move in the right direction.

Someone Who Understands

It's not enough that they sit and listen, nodding their head up and down so much that it might launch off into space. They put themselves in your shoes and see things from your perspective.

They will give you a real answer to a real problem, not just comfort you.

Okay, so you might have a person in mind that has all these redeeming qualities, and you are pondering the real question. **"How do I become friends with Oprah Winfrey?"**

There are seven billion people on this planet, including loads of them people that would encompass all these qualities and probably a heck of a lot more. Look hard enough and you will find them!

My Secret of Attraction

Okay, so you want to attract the greatest people to your life. Someone who cares, who will always be there for you, who motivates you, who is honest, and who understands and inspires you. That person is not Oprah Winfrey. There are seven billion people on this planet, and you did look really hard, but you still couldn't find them? Ready for my secret of attraction?

How about we start with YOU?

The answer is to aim to be the greatest version of yourself. The side effects of this will provide you with the relationships, working atmosphere and friends you seek, if not more. Become a person with those qualities yourself, and you will easily attract others with the same quality, or more, to your life.

It all starts with you. Not fate, or destiny, or luck, or even owning a mini-bar. At this point by now, you know what to do and what not to do to make people like you, but what about YOU liking yourself?

Remember, to be likable involves giving first. If you're always there for someone you love, there will be someone who is always there for you. If you're an inspiration to others, there will be someone who inspires you. If you're honest and trustworthy, you will attract honest and trustworthy people to your life. If you work on making yourself happy, your spouse and kids will be happy. Give first and you shall receive.

Is it really that simple? How dare I make you wait until almost the end of this book to tell you something so simple, and how dare I even call it, "My Secret of Attraction?"

Yes, it is my secret, and yes it is this simple. The question is, are you willing to do it? While you should know now how to get people to like you, and how to deal with the people that don't, no matter what, you need to look into how you can get to a place of liking yourself.

If you work on yourself first then everything else will work itself out.

"*Easier said than done!*" – is it what you're probably mumbling? That is exactly what one of my good friends, Eric, told me. He called me one day, and told me he was ready to divorce his wife. I gave him the exact advice above and suggested maybe he should work on himself first. Angry and frustrated, he said the following.

"I know you said that, but it's easier said than done. I'm not the problem. You don't know my wife. She is the problem. She complains all the damn time. She is not happy to see me. She gets angry easily. She argues over every damn little thing. She doesn't take care of the kids properly. She's the one who brought up divorce first, not me."

He went on for another five minutes talking about his wife. She was this, and she was that, *"I've tried my best to change her, but it's hopeless, I'm ready to give up,"* he concluded.

"Yes, Eric", I said, *"I only met your wife once at your wedding, and I don't know her personally. Maybe what you said is true. Maybe she's the problem. And I know you've tried your best to change her. But don't you see, trying to change her is so damn hard, a lot harder than changing*

yourself? Do you think that you're perfect and don't need to change a single thing?"

Silence.

"When was the last time you praised her, Eric?"

Silence.

"She doesn't have anything good to praise," he finally said.

"Start praising her, Eric. Try to look for the good in her. Tell her how great of a person she is. Tell her how beautiful she is, how great of a mom she is to your children, and mean it in every word you say. When you look for the good, you will start to see the good. When you talk about the good from her, you will draw out the good from her. But it all starts with YOU, Eric. Change yourself first. It's much easier than changing others. Make yourself a better husband, and you will see her become a better wife."

Eric agreed to give it some thought, and ended up

deciding to give it a try. Last time I checked, they were still married and he told me things were getting better. He started to see his wife as a woman he once dreamed about, and he started to see himself becoming a better husband and a better dad.

So, if you're feeling frustrated in a relationship with your loved ones—the ones that you can't simply cut out of your life like the other toxic people, how about starting with you? Make yourself a better person, and your loved ones will make themselves better because of you.

If you want to be friends with great people, work on improving yourself. Become a great person first. Then you won't need to try too hard, you won't need to find them or chase them. They will come to you.

***

<u>My Secret of Attraction:</u> It's much easier to change yourself. If you work on yourself first, everything else will work itself out.

***

Final Words

Life is not a popularity contest, at least in adult life. There are always going to be challenges with socializing, but if you are aware of what it means to be liked, how to be liked and how to use it, you will notice a pattern of unlimited rewards.

You should now know that saying yes is easy. There is no confrontation in saying yes, and the wimpy say yes all the time. You also know that it takes courage from a badass to say no. That badass will stand up and say no when needed. That badass will stand tall when surrounded by enemies. That badass is firm in front of the toxic people, but soft and kind toward people who need it. That badass is not afraid to admit their weakness and is willing to work on themselves. That badass is YOU. You have all the knowledge to become the likable badass you ever dreamed of.

You now understand that people yearn for validation, even yourself. Give it to them and you shall get yours. You realize how powerful a simple smile is. You know what to do first to make people interested in you. You know that life is not bunch of business transactions, and that we always need to get something in return first. You know it's easier to work on yourself than on others. You now know exactly how to make people to like you.

My friend, I wrote this book for you from the bottom of my heart, and I hope that you will take the principles provided to genuinely make people around you happy, and as a reward, you will be happy, and you will be the most likable person you ever dreamed of.

It won't happen overnight, but you have the know-how now. You just need to be self-disciplined enough to stick to it and see it through to the end. Remember, we are all guilty of being lazy, and it's up to you if you want to choose actions over words.

And for the enemies, we can always recall one or two assholes who made our lives hell, but instead of engaging, you now know how to use this as a motivation to become even more awesome than you already are.

Please, please, please don't waste your time on people who don't appreciate you, or the efforts you put in to satisfying their needs. For those people, use the principles I described in my other book, *"Secrets of Not Giving a F*ck."* Use your time and energy finding and attracting others who would lift you up and motivate you. Think about the things you can gain rather than the things that drain you.

I hope this book has revolutionized your mind, put things into perspective and given you great lessons on the power of likability.

Thank you for reading until the end. Time is not returnable or renewable, so trusting me with your time is really a privilege. It means a lot to me, probably more than you think. So THANK YOU!

This is not the end, but the beginning. It is time for you to become the best version of yourself.

So, go out there and show the world how much of a likable badass you are.

Bye for now, and take care!

Berger McDonald

***

If you like this book, please consider writing me a review! It's the only way to help me reach more readers. I read all the reviews and I look forward to reading yours! Thank you.

***

Check out my other books:

If you like audiobook, listen to the FREE audio sample of this book on my website at www.AwesomeHappyBadass.com/fck. You can also request a FREE copy of this full audiobook on my website as well. From time to time, Audible gives me free codes to give out to my readers. When they do, I'll give it to you to listen to it for FREE.

Badass Likability

***

Connect with me at

www.AwesomeHappyBadass.com

***

www.ingramcontent.com/pod-product-compliance
Lightning Source LLC
Chambersburg PA
CBHW071520080526
44588CB00011B/1501